I0132613

STILL CRAZY IN LOVE

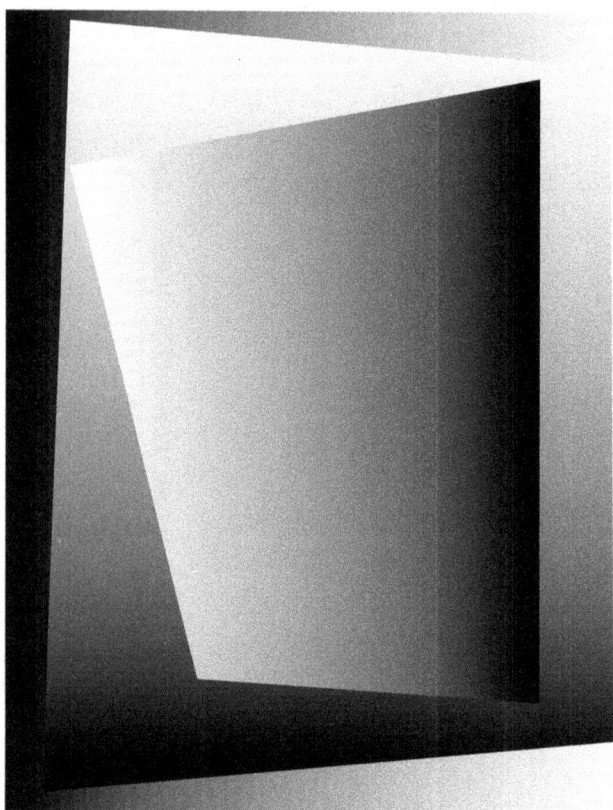

FOR LINDE

# STILL CRAZY
# IN LOVE

*poems*

Lito Tejada-Flores

WESTERN EYE PRESS

2011

*Still Crazy in Love*
is published by Western Eye Press,
a small independent press
(very small and very independent)
with a home base in
the Colorado Rockies
and an office
in Sedona Arizona.

© 2011 Lito Tejada-Flores
Western Eye Press
PO Box 1008
Sedona AZ 86339
1 800 333 5178
www.WesternEyePress.com
ISBN13: 978-0-941283-29-8

Book design and graphics by the author.
The type is Optima by Herman Zapf,
a 20th-Century classic

# CONTENTS

# IT MATTERS

Winter matters, not ski school:
windblasted beauty, hoarfrosted trees,
snowflakes drifting thru forest silence.
Skiing with you matters, not just skiing:
double exposure of winter & dance.
Perfect tracks don't matter, or poor ones.
Perhaps it matters that all tracks
are always erased?  Perhaps not?
It matters that you love me.


Spring matters, not taxes,
not snowmelt mud, not windy
gray days while the world wakes up.
New crocuses matter, stubborn beauty
of tulips, doubled under a last late snow.
Spring cleaning matters, & crab-apple blossoms
& wild asparagus.  Maybe it matters
what day the first hummingbird returns?
It matters that you love me.


Summer matters, not suntans:
evenings long with light, wood floors
warm to our feet in the early morning.
Thunder & lightning matter, rain & rainbows,
garden strawberries red right through.
Old fences matter, paved parking lots don't.
Do 4th of July picnics & fireworks matter?
Wild mushrooms do, & waistdeep wildflowers.
It matters that you love me

Autumn matters, not dead leaves:
singlepane windows etched in frost feathers,
heartbreak colors of forests on fire,
piñon smoke smells, & ice on puddles.
Politics doesn't matter, or profit or loss.
Each extra day of deeper orange & gold,
autumn's diehard beauty, seems to matter.
Getting wood in before it snows matters.
It matters that you love me.


Mountains matter, not tourists,
not téléphériques, not postcards,
but endless ranges, stacked in blue haze.
Adventures matter, record ascents don't.
It matters peaks are pointed, glaciers blue.
Elk herds matter, trophy hunters don't.
Quiet matters, but does loneliness?
Does difficulty, or daring really matter?
It matters that you love me.


Beauty matters, not money,
making beauty as much as living it.
Making a living matters less
than living in beauty. Happiness matters
& a few friends, full hearts, clear eyes.
True love matters most.
Maybe life matters, maybe not?
Your smile matters terribly.
It matters that you love me.

# SWEDISH HOUSES

a ballad for Linda

1

Come live with me in a brick red house,
on a high-hewn hill by the frozen sea,
in a house as red as the evening sun,
in a fire tight house, come live with me!

—A deep red house means an angry heart,
means words to tear our love apart,
means blows & tears & nights alone,
I'll never call this house my home!

2

Come live with me in a yellow gold house,
by a lonesome lake in a frozen land,
in a house as gold as ripened wheat,
as gold as the sun, come live with me!

—A yellow house means a greedy heart,
means money and things to keep us apart,
means bulging cupboards & an empty bed,
a yellow house is worse than red!

3

Come live with me in a sea green house,
on a storybook street in a tiny town,
in a house as green as the new spring grass,
or the winter sea, come live with me!

—A sea green house means a jealous heart,
means shadows to pull our love apart,
means fear to leave your love alone,
I'll call no sea green house my own!

4

Come live with me in a pale white house,
in a far off land by an empty beach,
a house as white as the sparkling sand,
or summer clouds, come live with me!

—A pure white house means an empty heart,
means a perfect dream to hold us apart,
means nothing is ever good enough,
a pure white house would kill our love!


5

So where will you live & be my love?
O tell me true & tell me now,
I'll build you the house your heart desires
where the world ends if you'll live with me.

—Then build me a house as blue as air,
robbin's egg light, mountain stream clear,
for blue means freedom, from fear, from care,
where my heart is free, I'll love you there.


*1 January 84  Sigtuna, Sweden*
*1 April 84  Düsseldorf, Germany*

# TRANSLATION

When I say: *I love you.*
it means: you are the first light
hitting the snowpeaks above town
making me smile every morning

When I say: *Where's the checkbook?*
or— *I'm going out to split more wood.*
or—*Looks like it's going to rain.*
it means: *I love you.*

When I say: *I love you.*
it means: you are the wind
shaking new aspen leaves in spring
making high noon bearable in summer
turning the forest floor gold in autumn

When I say: *I've lost my keys.*
or— *Why don't you put on some Mozart?*
or— *You should stop by the post office.*
it means: *I love you.*

When I say: *I love you.*
it means: how lucky I am
that you have a dimple in one cheek,
that your eyes sparkle in the dark,
that you are always hungry for beauty.

When I don't say anything at all
it also means: *I love you.*

WINTERWORDS    WINTERLOVE

1

stones
riverwashed,
tumbled
& ground,
—round &
polished,
silent
granite
spheres

words,
glacierground
compact
& polished,
—smooth &
hard,
eloquent
granite
sounds

2

2:00 AM
moonlit
night
moonlit
morning

under
cold stars
cold mountains
cold roof
cold quilt

warm arms
legs
hearts
tangled
          together

glowing
          embers

*10 December 87*

3

headlight
tunnel
piercing
mountains

4

roadside
deer
suicide squads
in ambush

snowing
one
whole
week—
six inches

graydawn
lake
no boats
no cars

max
no drifts
no powder
no point
no matter

forestfire
sunrise
behind
Monarch Pass

watching
avalanches
of fine
mist

first
flakes
thickening
into blizzard

cascade
down
black
cliffs

snowplastered
cows
hunkering
downwind

rogue
winter
out of
control
again

find
payphone
call
home—
    "I made it."

predictably
following
no one's
plans—

*Telluride/Crested Butte*
*5:00 am – 8:00 am, 11 December 87*

5

lost
under
an avalanche
of down
covers

your
tousled
head

your
subversive
smile

your
shining
eyes

warming
frosty
air

6

etchedglass
cloudfrost
spiderweb
icecrystal

morning
            window

shortest
day—
            dawn

trying
to look
out—

            are
peaks
still
there?

7

not
"beaten down
by beauty"
but
bouyed
up
    no
    other
    explanation
no
other
woman
    more
    beautiful
    every
    day
no
other
eyes
smile
    at
    so much
    beauty
    every
    day

8

white
walls
old
bones

empty
walls
midwinter
light

bare
walls
simple
beauty

quiet
walls
quiet
music

simple
walls
simple
love

# DAWN INVENTORY

half awake in
half light
        first light
first thoughts
taking inventory
in grayblue dawn:

our mountains:
hiding their heads
in cloud blankets
healing avalanche scars
in mist & snow
welcoming an
overdue storm

our porch:
windchimes
banging madly
windhorses
galloping in place
skis stacked
in untidy heaps

our bed:
pillows piled
two deep
safe harbor for
foolish dreams
warm tangle
under the duvet

our life together:
sometimes too hard
mostly too busy
often too beautiful
always too perfect

*3 February 89*      *Telluride*

minimalism


small
    house
        large
            view


beautiful
    valley
        beautiful
            woman


few
    things
        one
            love


many
    choices
        only
            you

NIGHTIME

DREAMTIME

DAWNHOUSE

DAWNSKIES

GRAYPINKS

PINKBLUES

DAWNPEAKS

EASTLIGHT

WHITEWALLS

DOWNCOVER

LOVESFACE

LOVESMILE

DAYDREAMS

DREAMDAYS

winter's last gasp, grasp-
ing at last flakes, thick white
blanket pulled over drygrass,
white aspenlace, white cliffs,
lightweight flakes, lost
flakes, falling in slowmotion,
      pillowbound, quiltcovered
      your soft sleepsmile under
      layers of goosedown, dreams,
falling in slowmotion, whiteflecked air,
spindrift dawn drifting upvalley,
mist rags caught on mountain walls,
pilgrim sun pushing across
eastern passes through thick cloud,
winter's comeback, doublepane diorama,
inside the paperweight, or out,
softfocus white forests climbing
into snowsky, borderless white.
      deep in drifts of pillows
      your wakeup smile starts
      a second dawn.

*29 March 90*

# SEOUL SUNSET

Tweenlight turns the Seoul sky insideout, iridescent,
bleeds purple out of city lights upward into low clouds:
neon nighttime warming up, & you're not here to see it.

Rooftop religion, red neon crosses, campfires in mist.
Seoul is a sermon about hard work & the pointlessness
of hard work, because you're not here to share it.

Rivers of neon flow down narrow streets, drunk
on sojou & rice wine & words even children can read
Koreans dream a Chinese past into a Japanese future.

On every corner tent pubs glow orange, pepper hot
pre-MacDonalds fastfood parties, black silhouettes
gesture against the canvas; the night shift eats & runs.

Koju jang & OB beer, strong spice of a too tough life,
but across the border, north, night is a pure pitch black
& it wouldn't matter if you were there, or existed at all

*An Yang,*
*May 1990*

# WINTER MORNING

Last leaves
first snowfall
long late
autumn's
forest alchemy:
green to gold
suddenly it's
winter's turn:
gold to silver

      Last dreams
      first light
      dark house
      dark peaks
      against pale
      eastern sky
      & suddenly
      your smile's
      gold & silver

            Last coffee
            & first light
            new day
            new season
            frostfeathers
            icesculpture
            & suddenly
            solid peaks
            turn to lace

                  First / last
                  early / late
                  autumn / winter
                  mountain / desert
                  black coffee
                  & foamed milk
                  but only your
                  early morning
                  smile counts     *22 October 90*

LINDE—

It's statistically unlikely that the curve
of your hip beside me in bed is unique
in a world of five billion plus

It's emotionally improbable that I
should love you more today than yesterday
(and more yesterday than the day before)

It's hard to believe that you are so much
more beautiful now than you were
when we met, 15, 16, 17 years ago

It's unlikely, improbable, hard to believe
& true


*5 December 90*

# NARROW ESCAPES

Listening over breakfast to the story
of a friend misdiagnosed with breast cancer—
life's full of narrow escapes, until finally,
one day, one doesn't quite make it.
My narrowest escape?  Well, of course
there were moments in the mountains:
storms, avalanches pouring over our heads,
ropes hung up, lightning charring summits,
but really my closest call must have been
almost not meeting you, life without Linde
—unthinkable.


*10 December 90*
*Denver*

# CHRISTMAS POEM

Your two goodmorning eyes
beam me up to secret summits
where I often stay all day
above a sea of clouds, *Nebelmeer,*
*la mer de nuages de la realité,*
descending back to valley bottom
only after a red desert sunset's
lit the Utah border, burned on west,
your at last tired eyes shut tight
dreamwatching endless stars
above our midnight mountain house

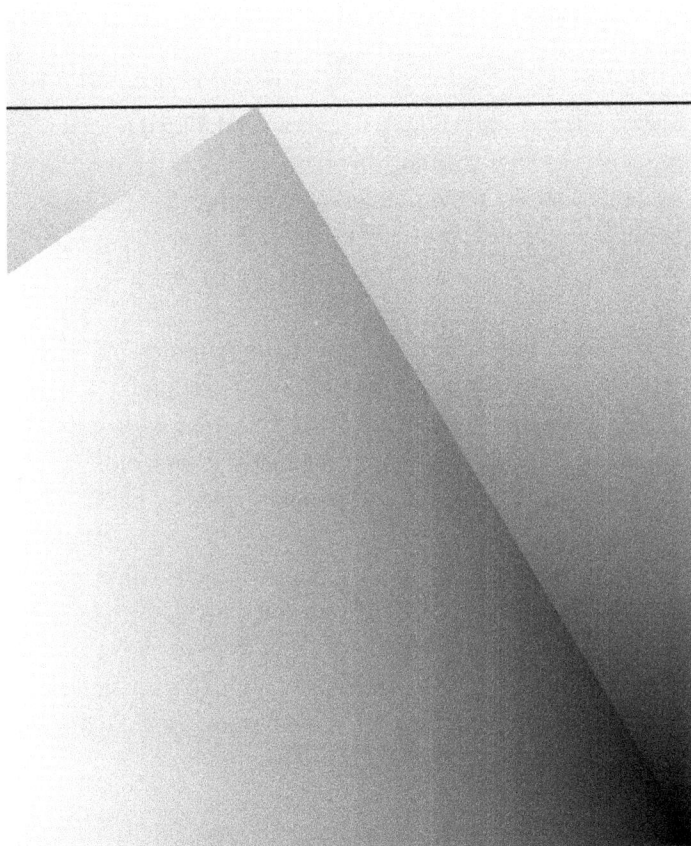

# HINTS OF SPRING

Spring hits the high country unannounced, one day
we find ourselves yawning in lemon sunshine, the next
soaked by slushy snow. Winter's wounds start to heal:
knees unbend, the corners of flower beds melt out,
for a moment mud has its reason, rebirth its season.

Spring fever ambushes us in supermarket parking lots
foothill ranches fill up with calves, like us too tired
to get up and run around. It'll be here any day we say,
forgetting this new valley grass is already a week old.
Without warning winter counterattacks, takes us back.

Lets us go again. Seasons exchanging prisoners while
the world wakes up from war, turns off the TV, rubs
dazzled dimmed eyes, stretches, sighs. We dream
of spring's arrival & it's already here: your hip's soft hollow
in our midnight bed, dawns dark with storm, bright with love.

*5 March 91*

## ALBA FOR LINDE

early AM blues—
the sky I mean
& mountain shapes
navyblue shadows
bluestone
      bluecliff
blueblack
      bluegray
blueday dawning
in a blue window

4 AM flowers—
columbine shadows
nodding sleepeyed
in a blue window
yellowblues
      pinkblues
      purpleblues
cloudhorses
stampeding west
running from dawn
dawnwind shaking
aspen shadows

early AM thoughts—
a sleeptight house
with blue windows
daylight wrestling
thru high passes
my truelove safe
under bluedown
drifts of shadow
a sleeptight quilt
blueday dawning
      bright

*21 May 91*

# SANTA FE ALBA

Santa Fe's stupid without you, you know—
New Mexico' wide adobe screen goes blank
& sunrise preforms its tricks to an empty house.
Under a redgold atomic cloudfire sky I walk
from one plastered room called sleep into
another one called waking up.  It is not so
interesting here in the real world without you;
& even the best espresso machine in all
the southwest can't reconcile me to
even this one morning without you.


*October 91*

# THE INSOMNIAC NIGHT


Soft in the insomniac night
under a rain of moondrops
crashing silent on our silent valley
sidelit eastside by hints of dawn
nightwind rattling aspens & chimes,
slowly shredding the prayer flag
into prayers, soft in early lateness
flashbacks of our twentyear love
float downvalley, freezeframe
on white cotton windowshades
flicker & dissolve.

                    you hold me
in the round silk corral
of your sleeptight arms
sleeping on my shoulder
under a sea of down, under
a moonstorm of memories
Bear Valley, Stinson Beach,
firstgold of San Juan autumns
firstwhite of Swiss winters
geraniums behind lace curtains
redblossom trees New Zealand spring
summers waistdeep in wildflowers
your eyes' apprenticeship
to beauty, image by image,
film by film, year after year.
your silvertoned laughter
your grownup body still
growing lovelier day by day,
year after year

you hold me
soft in the insomniac night
in a sleepy circle of memories
an embrace of old embraces
behind my shoulder you breathe
clouds across the moon.
I wonder if this is the second act
or the third act of our lovestory.
I know it's not the same old story
I tell myself it does not need
a last act, a resolution, a curtain
I tell myself it's raining moonlight
outside, blowing clouds
I get up to watch the mountains
to write you this story
of my insomniac night.


*16 June 92*
*Telluride*

# DREAMING

1
you are a dream
that talks back
looks back
touches back
hugs back
loves back

2
you are a dream
of a dream
no one would dare
to dream

3
you are a dream
that dreams back
perhaps you
dreamed me
perhaps we
can dream the rest
of our life together

4
you are a dream
of beauty &
intelligence &
sex &
friendship &
imagination
that no one
dreamed but
that happened
anyway

5
you are
my dream
but your own
person

6
you are not
a dream


*24 June 92*

# UNFINISHED POEM

I haven't finished loving you
it's a long slow business
true love
one can't just rush it
get it over with
& move on
sometimes I do it right
sometimes not
sometimes I think I'm getting better
sometimes I think it doesn't matter
loving you is what I do
it's what I want to do
it takes a long time
I haven't finished loving you

I haven't finished touching you
it's a long beautiful country
this body of yours
it changes with the seasons
with the years
with moods & weather
it gets more beautiful
with the years
with moods & weather
it makes me always
happier
I haven't finished touching you

I haven't finished writing
this poem for you
it's a long hard job
to say what I feel
I don't think I'll ever finish
I don't think I'm supposed to

*Thanksgiving 92*

# ADOBE DAWN

i
Adobe dawn
dyes the sky &
morning monochrome
retreats one window
at a time
mountains asleep
beneath a single star,
the world turns
slowly in its sleep,
eastern shoulders
under a blanket
of warm color,
first light first,
then first pink
salmon peach lemon
early autumn colors
slow sky stucco
wind wakes up
juniper shadows shake
piñon creaks
under this weight
of adobe dawn.

ii
Under shadow covers
in a shadow bed
a breathing shadow
among so many shadows
here at fingers' finding
night's last silence
dawn's first form
your new   old   timeless
body beside me,
shadow locked landscape
waiting for light,
skin landscape
bone landscape
dreaming of dawn,
waiting for a poet,
a photographer, a lover,
your landscape
your adobe dawn
your lover

*September 93*
*Santa Fe,*

COLD MOUNTAIN

VALENTINE

ONE POEM

TWO VIEWS

Cold
Mountain
isn't
cold

dawns
crimson
then
gold

susnets
warm
wide
long

bells
wind
equal
song

peaks
tower
clouds
roam

Cold
Mountain
feels
home

deer
antelope
dogs
us

joy
work
love
peace

| Cold | Mountain | isn't | cold |
|------|----------|-------|------|
| dawns | crimson | then | gold |
| susnets | warm | wide | long |
| bells | wind | equal | song |

| peaks | tower | clouds | roam |
|-------|-------|--------|------|
| Cold | Mountain | seems | home |
| deer | antelope | dogs | us |
| joy | work | love | peace |

*13 February 96*

an honor guard of bluebirds whistles
the sun back over eastern mountains
dawn tiptoes thru our bedroom
lets sleeping dogs lie, discovers
your smile adrift on a sea of down
pillow waves, bed's harbor.
Dawn's alchemy
in night's darkroom's done,
the landscape slips back
from black-and-white to color.


*6 February 96*

# IT'S MIDNIGHT

it's midnight, it's morning
it's a dream, it's a warning
it's the look in your eye
it's the sun in the sky
it's dawn, it's gone
it will never come back
it's the past, it's tomorrow
it's beauty, it's sorrow
it's the way that we live
it's the love that we give
it's the wind, it's the sand
it's the rock, it's the land
it's the west
it's the west—

it's better, it's worse
it's a blessing, a curse
it's the night, it's the light
it's love, it's despair
it's a song in the air
it's a song, it's a prayer
it's you, it's me
it's the world outside
it's the love that we share
it's me, it's you
it's you, it's me

*April 97*
*Crestone*

Sans toi, le soir n'a pas de sens
Sans toi, les heures avancent
            en boitant, en titubant, en rampant
            c'est lent le temps
            triste et lent
Sans toi, ce repas n'a pas de gout
            pas de tout
La nuit, la neige, les arbres
            aux bras verts vides grands ouverts
            t'attendent
L'hiver t'attend pour commencer
            pour recommencer
            pour être vrai
L'hiver aussi a besion de toi
            exactement comme moi


14 janvier 98
Ajax Tavern, Aspen

INVENTORY


a valley haunted by rainbows
a house haunted by happiness
a heart haunted by your smile
why haunted? why not enchanted?
why not both? Yes, both!

*29 August 98*

# BRIGHT ANGEL

Back from the canyon—
the Colorado has cut
a canyon-shaped idea
through the sediments
of daily life: an Arizona
of unpaid bills, a Utah
of half finished projects
great unconformity
of dreams & days.

Bright angel—
we don't have to leave
this river, take out,
deflate our rafts &
go back to work,
carving these canyons,
smoothing this rock
is real work too.

Bright angel—
let me love you
as long & hard as water
wearing through stone.
Bright angel—
love me in flash floods,
secret reflecting pools,
side canyons, waterfalls,
safe eddies turning gold
in predawn light.

Together we can polish
the dark fireborn bedrock
of our lives into strange
& wondrous  shapes

# R I V E R     C A N Y O N     L O V E

Gliding down long reflecting tongues
glassy dreamlike swells
toward the exploding waves of our bed

After each rapid
the stillwater of your smile
Day by day drifting, dropping
down the long canyon of our love
nothing is ever the same
day by day everything changes:
river & rock, sky & water
there is always color before dawn
there is always color after sunset
there is always beauty
whenever we look for it

This trip of ours is longer
than John Wesley Powell's
this canyon grander
we are each other's boats
we never have to take out

At ears' end in the near night I hear
A river, hear it whisper, hear
A horizontal waterfall's water
Falling, canyonwall echoes growl
Into silence, water falling
Out of mountains toward the sea
Whispering thru dark crosscut
Contour lines, upcanyon only cliffs
& waterfalls, & down, downvalley
Downcanyon, downcountry, those
Geocenturies thousand footyears
Deep above tomorrow's sea

                    river ride, river run
San Miguel, Dolores, Colorado, small
At first, great at last, night's waterfall
Falling sideways west across the map
Headwaters dark dream whispering
In the narrow night at ears' end


I can hear it here at night's end
Day's done in a wide warm bed beneath
Mountains, under falls, each drop
Dreams of the sea, hushing between walls
In the dreamcanyon night, hear it fall
Out of heart's hearing, there at ears' end.

Here at heart's end in our dear narrow bed
Your shoulder rises, hip dips beside me
Sleeping thru the canyonwalled night
Avalanche snowmelt & waterfall
Ripple & rill, rapid & eddy, dam & spillway
& my thoughts dropping drop by drop
Toward your sea, your last beach & each
Sand grain each tomorrow, each smile
Each new life, dawn, day we share here
At heart's end, ears' end, night's end
Nine thousand feet above the sea, each
Drop of love riversung at ears' end
In the near & whispering night.

A four-cornered five-o'clock sunrise scatters
pink in all directions: east, west, north, south.
Today is the last longest day of the century,
high-desert dawn hung with pink gauze curtains.

Borges was not the first to note that someday
even the last memory of this too rosy dawn
will disappear. Sooner, I'd say, rather than later.
Those garish colors already gone, fugitive pastels....

Everything changes but beauty lingers in the heart
long after whatever's beautiful's gone.
Color comes and goes, dreams of color stay.

How can the very same dawn masquerade
as a lesson in impermanence and in forever?
Time troubles us—truest of fictions.

# SOLSTICE SUNSET

Between the last shortest day
and the last longest night
of the century, the world
blushes at its own beauty

Our color-blind dogs sit
watching the last light
paint the peaks, without
calenders, without centuries

We are as quiet as our dogs
wind blows the prayer flags
we see snow, suffering, happiness

Dogs, friends, strangers,
tomorrow we start our climb
together toward the light

1

Uninhabited castles of unmortared rock
How do they stick together? What holds
them up? Is it the stubborn grass? Green
tongues licking up alpine slopes

into gullies of redgold scree, gouged,
sliding forever downhill: unpolished
unquiet rock, distant echoes off
canyon walls, distant rockfall rumbles,

dust flies, settles. Down here flowers
fill a six-week summer with color.
Paintbrush paint the valley flanks: pinks

and oranges duke it out in profusion.
Clouds tear past these peaks. What really
holds these spires up, if not love?


*14 July 96*
*Yankee Boy Basin*

. . . . . . . . . . . . . . . . . .

2

Twenty years ago your body was a wilderness,
today it has become my favorite landscape:
storms & sunsets & earthquakes still pass through
your territory: hills & hollows, bone, skin.

I have explored your body's backcountry so often,
by now I know all your paths & passes,
your shortcuts, box canyons, arroyos, playas,
I have memorized your vistas, admired your dawns.

Your body is still a wilderness. I can wrap my arms
around your slender waist more easily than my mind,
I still wonder if I can really cross your deserts

of smiling skin, if there are secrets there I've never
learned, quiet secret places I've stumbled across
by accident, then lost, & will never find again....

*21 January 97*
*Aspen*

. . . . . . . . . . . . . . . . . . . .

3

Dawn creeps over the mountains wrapped in snow.
The white earth says hello to the white sky.
A runaway locomotive of happiness pulls
our white bed forward into another day:

Pillows filled with snow, sky full of feathers,
our house anchored in the outwash of canyons,
your delicate head anchored in the hollow of my shoulder.
Once again, winter whitewashes the land.

Happiness happens, like snow, but thicker, deeper,
storm after season after year, piling up
in drifts around us: pillows, comforters of happiness.

It never stops. I wake with my arms around you
and it doesn't matter if the sun ever makes it
over those eastern peaks and through our window.


*23 February 97*
*Crestone*

. . . . . . . . . . . . . . . . . .

4

Winter winds its white rope of shrinking days
tighter around our house, our hearts.
Fresh sheets spill down out of the mountains...
The big tent of the western sky sags lower,

brushes the hills, the juniper, rabbitbrush, ricegrass.
Air thickens into snow, daylight into halflight.
Already Indian summer seems like a dream—clouds
floating through a sky of transparent warmth,

an autumn's inheritance squandered on small things,
last leaves long spent. It was a dream. So is winter.
We'll wake in a few months when the colors return

with the cranes, put away our boots, gloves, sweaters,
unpack our lives, wonder: What next? What now?
Love is the answer. Winter is not the question.


*14 November 97*
*Crestone*

. . . . . . . . . . . . . . . . . . . .

5

Your quiet breathing beside me in the dawn:
small waves of happiness splashing up
on the wintergray beach of a new day,
sand of a new day, empty, waiting

for first footsteps, first thoughts.
In the distance, mountains, winterclouds, work.
In the distance, out of sight not mind,
runaway horses of hatred are galloping

across the world, stampeding, trampling.
I don't even want to turn on the radio:
car bombs, war crimes, massacres,

a rollercoaster of money, greed, ambition.
This morning your breathing beside me
is my first and last line of defense.

*2 December 97*
*Aspen*

. . . . . . . . . . . . . . . . . .

6

December far from home, waiting for more snow
missing our dogs, saving pennies, saying: soon,
one more year, and knowing: next year is now, last
year too, always now, this is as far as we're going,

this present moment, lit by your smile, full, empty.
Here. Now. I will never reach the bottom of this
mountain, never finish this novel, the future is too far,
the present just big enough to hold these 14 lines for you.

Each ski turn is my first and my last, each snowflake,
each storm, each student, each story, each corny joke...
Each time you smile, this crowded present moment

expands, the universe expands, breathes, smiles back.
You are December, you are home, your smile
a year round summer solstice lighting this midwinter sky.

*9 December 97*
*Aspen*

. . . . . . . . . . . . . . . . . . .

7

Your nakedness falls on my mind
a summer storm out of an empty blue sky.
I am never ready, never prepared for so much beauty.
I am always ready, always prepared to love you.

Your two hands touch my hands
two birds bearing gifts of green leaves.
You are the gift and the giver, you give me
morning & evening, mountains & deserts, moon & stars.

Beauty & love can't be weighed, tallied, traded,
they just happen, like weather like winter like sunlight,
unearned rewards for imaginary lives I can't recall.

Beauty & love can't be explained, justified, understood,
only shared & treasured. These are my treasures:
your nakedness, your hands, your smile, your laughter.

*25 December 97*
*Cold Mountain*

. . . . . . . . . . . . . . . . . .

8

The year begins before dawn, deep under goosedown,
halfasleep, you throw your arms around me in the dark,
dense fog throws its arms around our house, our peaks,
darkness dissolves into whiteness, fog into snow

and back again, white earth into white sky into first light
and back again, directionless light lights up a lack of stuff:
landscape and landform nowhere seen, nowhere felt.
I feel you beside me, a sleeping girl in a white room.

This is all I need, not winter, not mountains, not you
but waking up beside you, not last night, not tomorrow
but night becoming day, today dissolving into today,

now into still more now, the present moment into still
more present moment, sleeping into waking into hugging,
not life but living, not you, not love, but loving you.


*1 January 98*
*Cold Mountain*

. . . . . . . . . . . . . . . . . .

9

| | |
|---|---|
| Breathing in | I feel myself breathe in |
| breathing out | I am aware of breathing out |
| | |
| breathing in | I am light air wind cloud |
| breathing out | I am solid heavy mountain earth |
| | |
| breathing in | I feel the wind breathing in the trees |
| breathing out | I am aware of the mountains breathing |
| | |
| breathing in | I feel the earth below me, supporting me |
| breathing out | I feel the mountains supporting the sky |
| | |
| breathing in | I am also loving you |
| breathing out | I am happy |
| | |
| breathing in | I can't separate breathing from loving you |
| breathing out | I can't separate mountain from wind from you |
| | |
| breathing in & out | I am just breathing in and out |
| loving you | I am just loving you |

*24 August 98*
*Crestone*

. . . . . . . . . . . . . . . . . . .

10

In another room you are already
asleep, in another life I never
met you, in another you leave me
for a Hungarian violinist, not

a gypsy, an aristocrat. But in
this life, in this house, tonight,
the auspicious stars, the moon
behind cirrocumulus curtains,

dogs panting quietly in their sleep—
everything conspires toward
an unstable perfection, equally

impossible to justify, understand,
explain. Your quiet breathing
all that keeps this world intact..

*4 September 98*
*Cold Mountain*

. . . . . . . . . . . . . . . . . . . .

11

Autumn multiplied out of mind
a forest of smoldering flickering embers
each leaf retells the same story
in a thick improbable accent of color

Autumn seems endless, ends anyway
an abrasion of weeks and days and
wind turns color into loss
wind sweeps up, snow hides evidence

Autumn ends, love doesn't
your smiles light up these lost days
each smile burns brighter

tells a new story in new colors
a new reason for falling in love
with the same woman


*16 October 98*

. . . . . . . . . . . . . . . . . .

12

No poet ever wrote: "You are like
an elevated freeway in the dawn, like
a high tension power line lighting up
distant cities." I won't either. You aren't.

I watch you sleeping under down covers,
I can't say you are like the moon, like clouds,
I realize I am a man without metaphors:
You are like nothing else in this life.

You represent nothing else, you are, you do.
You fill places inside me I never suspected,
free my mind from logic, my heart from regret.

I drive off into blackness, starless, wet,
no dawn today, no distant cities light up,
there will be no morning this morning.


*26 October 98*
*Crestone 4:00 AM*

. . . . . . . . . . . . . . . . .

13

Winter is waking up in the high country
it won't stumble downcanyon for days
dawn and dusk paint snow peaks pink
valley floor stays stubborn yellow

I touch your back for luck, fire up
the espresso machine, watch the sky
bleaching away from black mountains
house and heart turned east, waiting

Waiting for winter to fall downhill
into our lives, for this white future
to become tomorrow, today, right now

Winter wipes away everything unfinished
fresh snow erases each false start
winter freezes only fingers, not hearts


*24 November 98*
*Cold Mountain*

. . . . . . . . . . . . . . . . . .

14

Windhorses sleeping out of the wind
indoors, far from the sky, no prayers
tonight but the world will be okay
Prayers for all sentient beings don't

guarantee happiness, a lack of prayers
doesn't guarantee suffering either
Life goes on: blue, white, red, green
and yellow prayers, poised, ready...

History is the story of sentient beings
getting beaten up, a long sad story
without a happy ending, but history

is a hoax, true love is the revisionist
rewriting every page to come out right
stampeding windhorses into motion.

*December 98*
*Aspen*

. . . . . . . . . . . . . . . . . .

15

A sky full of stars not snow, a moon
unprotected by clouds, good weather
when we want bad, storms sliding by
on a runaway jet stream, empty weather.

Weather for waiting, but for what?
we are already here, already in love
already ready to write off winter
an innocent mistake, a sometime season.

Enough stars to fill a poem, enough
kisses to replace each snowflake that
never falls, more than enough love.

Empty weather is a gift, together
we can create either winter or freedom
from winter, together imagine spring.


*December 98*
*Aspen*

16

Today is the last day of one life
the first of another, days without end
that always end, our days are numbered,
of course, but the numbers don't add up.

Today is not just yesterday plus one,
not just almost tomorrow, today is it,
all we've got, all we need, all there is,
today is either enough or too much.

You are too much and just enough,
you are here today, and today
is the best of all days because of you.

Today is the only day of our life.
Today is the first and last day.
Today never ends.


*December 98*
*Aspen*

. . . . . . . . . . . . . . . . . . .

17

Haunted by blue skies, winter waits
for a sign, a red dawn, a single
lenticular cloud snagged on a summit
wind whistling out of the southwest

Clock more reliable than calendar
days merely shorter not colder
the long year throws its last days away
December dusks come early and quick

Christmas waits like a snare
baited with white memories
no gift of snow this year

you are the only gift I'll get
you are the only gift I need
winter can wait, and will

. . . . . . . . . . . . . . . . . .

18

moon almost full,
dawn almost here,
it's almost spring,
house almost silent,

you're almost awake,
I'm almost asleep
in your arms, heartbeat
breath, almost the same,

in disappearing darkness
I count everything I love:
you, our dogs, our house, you,

life together, our work,
you, mountain sunrise,
you—almost too much


*1 March 99*
*Cold Mountain*

. . . . . . . . . . . . . . . . . .

19

bent double under our burden of happiness
we put our heads down, push into the wind
the San Luis valley is blowing away
air full of sand dunes, no sky left

sitting squirming under the world's sorrow
we turn on the radio, listen to the news
like drunks reaching for another bottle
why this daily research into despair?

mountaintops fly snowscarves in the wind
spring still trying to negotiate a truce
this weather makes prayer flags productive

but does it help? seems almost unfair
selfish, to hold onto so much happiness
we want to share it & don't know how


*9 April 99*
*Cold Mountain*

20

beauty falls down out of the sky
onto the tin roof of our house
this San Luis sky spills snowflakes
virga cloud wisps, rain & rainbows

light tumbles down out of a late sky
into our plaza, into our hearts
this San Luis light gets inside of things
lights them from the inside out, glows

buried under gifts we ask each other:
why? how? how did we get here? how? why?
we know there is no answer

we know this place would be just as beautiful
if we were not here to see it, our lives
just as magical if someone else were living them


*9 April 99*
*Cold Mountain*

. . . . . . . . . . . . . . . . . .

21

You wrap your smile tightly around me,
a down quilt on a frozen starry night.
You leave clues everywhere, all day long,
I should be able to figure this one out:

I am baffled by your beauty, it hides
in all the corners and cupboards of afternoon,
the evening sky full of clouds, full of colors,
your evening smiles full of clouds, light, colors.

I have almost deciphered your secret,
almost but not quite, my solutions crumble
under the weight of your eyes, my reasoning

is circular, only leads me back to your smile:
all my explanations of your beauty
crumble under the reality of your beauty.


*18 April 99*
*Cold Mountain / Houston*

. . . . . . . . . . . . . . . . . . .

22

Under a million stars
two more, your eyes
Beneath dark mountains
pale dunes, your hips

Creeks run into the sand
thirsty earth, drinking, drinking
Light bleeds over the peaks
hungry heart, gulping beauty

You are the last darkness
covering the slow retreat
of the last few stars

You are the first light
lighting a white room
making morning real


23 September 99

. . . . . . . . . . . . . . . . .

23

*Káyeh Hózhóní, "land of beauty all around"*

Beauty gets lost in the eye of the beholder
In the artist's eye it multiplies, expands
Beauty is not just a gift from the land
or a filter we use to look at the land

Beauty is a collaboration, a creation, a verb
Living in a land of beauty all around,
taking care of that land, praising it
with silence, time, attention

Káyeh Hózhóní is not the promised land
Can't get there in a fancy car, can't buy
a pass or a postcard, can't sell it either

Land of beauty all around…I live there
with you, I wake up there, looking east
Together we have created all this beauty

# GETTING UP, MAKING COFFEE

A crescent moon and Venus, low in the east
a heart shaped rock by the door
the first separation of dark mountains against dark sky
farther south, even paler, sky softens
a dark double lenticular cloud
floats above Médano Pass
double shadows on an empty sky
only a few stars left now
somewhere else first stars are reappearing
somewhen else these very stars will reappear
somewhere else it's already tomorrow
but here it's always today
still somewhen else haunts us:
the future fighting its way into the past
the past slamming the door to the future
the present trying to become truly present
we're almost there, almost here, almost now
it's dawn now, or at least pre-dawn
or at least post-night
dawn declares a truce
a space filling up with light
overflowing, expanding, breathing
the world breathes out, we breathe in
it is almost the hour of coffee and kisses
soon we will fall back
into the fiction of the new year
or new century or new millennium
as though numbers on a cosmic odometer
really ticked over together
the mountains will remind us that change is slow
the weather will argue that it's fast
true love will put change in its place
love, happiness, beauty, inextricably tangled
anger, hatred, brutality, only distant rumors
of distant shadows, fading
in an expanding circle of light.

*31 December 99  Cold Mountain*

# SUMMER STORMS

Summer monsoon storms scrub the air, the crags,
a full moon polishes them while we sleep.
In four hours I'll wake up again,
cheer the sun as it summits eastern peaks,

bring you coffee in bed, kiss you awake, wonder
if I'm still dreaming, dreaming a life or living a dream
or both, or maybe asking the wrong question
about the right woman, in the right place.

In your eyes, these mountains grow more beautiful,
in your arms, life makes even more sense,
in your smile, morning finds its meaning.

I don't know if our valley, our mountains, our bedroom
would be as perfect without this midnight  housekeeping
or if our love is moving mountains while we sleep.


*18 July 2000*
*Cold Mountain*

# COLD MOUNTAIN DECEMBER

### 1
sunrise staggers over the peaks
burdened with too much color
drunk on crimson clouds
from the east, bearing gifts

### 2
chamisa, rabbit brush, frost diamonds
the backlit foreground of another morning
no man's land, every man's land
below sleeping peaks

### 3
cottonwoods cluster by roadside
bare branches finger the winter sky
ice crystal clouds above the peaks
long rips in pure blue

### 4
one and a half degrees
must be winter, December 21st
today the sun starts north
today we drive home

### 5
sleeping house under sleeping peaks
writing in the espresso-dark night
everything good I write
is about you & for you

# CHANSON DE QUÉBEC

*Tu es mon rêve, le seul, le vrai*
*Tu es ma cinquième vérité*
*L'automne, l'hiver, le printemps, l'été*
*Tu es ma cinquième vérité*

*Quand je suis loin de toi*
*La vie manque de vie,*
*Tournant sur son axe*
*La terre ralentit,*
*Chaque nuit se prolonge*
*A l'infinie,*
*Le matin s'éternise*
*Sous des nuages gris,*
*Les jours se suivent*
*Le coeur s'ennuie,*
*Sans toi dans me bras*
*La vie manque de vie*

*Tu es mon rêve, le seul, le vrai*
*Tu es ma cinquième vérité*
*L'automne, l'hiver, le printemps, l'été*
*Tu es ma cinquième vérité*

*25 janvier 92*

LOVE IS ....


love is a lens
that focuses
all the beauty in the world
at one spot
in one person
you

love is an alembic
that distills
all the emotions in your heart
into one emotion,
pure happiness
pure Linde

love is a formula
that calculates
everything, the sum total
of all that matters,
the impossible sum
of all that counts
equals you


*28 December 2002*

# PREDAWN CRESTONE

1
Midnight over mountains
under mountains
all the world's colors
are resting just over
the earth's curve
They'll be back on duty
at 6AM
in the eastern sky

2
My thoughts follow you
from room to room
through our house
through my heart
your beauty parts the cold air
pushes cold thoughts aside
icebreaker parting ice-cold seasons
opening a channel
for warm thoughts

# MAY FIRST

Under mountains as vast as stars
under stars as infinite as lost thoughts,
the only thoughts I can rescue from
the wreckage of yesterday, of today,

of five minutes ago, are thoughts of you:

You ransom back these mountains from
a greedy night sky, from an indifferent world,
from a future impossible to trust.
                              I trust

your smile more than all the experts on TV
even though I never watch TV, more than
all the disembodied voices on the radio,

more than you can guess, though you can surely
guess what I'm thinking, writing these lines, late,
under mountains lit by dreams, by moonlight.


*1 May 2003*

# THE CENTER OF THINGS

At the center of so much movement, stillness
at the center of all this chaos, calm
at the center of so much noise, silence
at the center, behind all this hatred, love

Where is it? the thought with no afterthought?
the day with no yesterday, no tomorrow?
no more running away? no more running toward?
How do we get there? travelers without a map

At the center of the spinning spiral year
in the middle of an endless standstill day
a circle of infinite radius whose center

is everywhere: life looking for the center.
You are that center, the quiet center
of my circling thoughts, my circling arms.

# FULL MOON THOUGHTS.

after midnight, under mountains
the full moon has scrubbed
the soft southwest sky
bare of yesterday's clouds

under this same full moon
silent sand dunes
wait for nothing special
the earth turns

somewhere out there
coyotes whisper & whistle & whine
no louder than your breathing

my hand on your hip
you turn, the earth turns,
true love is the axis

*12 July 2006, 3:00 am*

# THE BIG QUESTIONS

If the question is death
the answer is life

If the question is life
the answer is love

If the question is love
the answer is you


*14 December 2007*

## NUESTRA CAMA

nuestra cama, una isla calma
en el flujo del tiempo
las mil y una cosas
días, dramas, deseos
actos, acontecimientos
problemas, propuestos,
listado demasiado largo
de una vida demasiado corta
resuelto
en nuestra cama

7 May 2010

*3:00 AM, Lago Carrera*

the steady chorus of waves
quietly noisy, slapping, sighing
the minimalist moon, climbing
crescent over Argentina:
20-watt moon bulb can't
light up the black ink sky
above our black ink lake
can't make glaciers
glow in the dark

sleepless in a sleeping cabin
sleeping dog, sleeping love
sheepskin & down covers
warm milk at 3:00 am
sleepyheaded search
for driftwood poems
sticks tossed up on
tomorrow's marble beach

tomorrow is never
as far away
as yesterday

*1 March 2008*

# LOOKING FOR BEAUTY

Looking for beauty, you become more beautiful
And you are always looking for beauty.
Looking for beauty, you always find it:
sudden sunset alchemy across the western sky

the base metal of leaden clouds
catching fire, transmuted into gold
but gold alone isn't beauty.
These once-in-forever colors

only catch at the heart
when they are heartfelt.
You feel every stab of beauty

And give it back,
magnified and
distilled.


*31 August 2003*

# THE GEOMETRY OF BEAUTY

1
in the simple geometry
of beauty
your eyes
replace parallel lines
looking for infinity
your small &
perfect breasts
are necessary &
sufficient conditions
to prove any theorem
the isosceles triangle
of your sex &
the infinite radius
of your smile
are the axioms
I start from
& return to


2
between the chaos & cruelty of the past
& the high-tech disasters of the future
between the safe brutality of socialism
& the insecure brutality of capitalism
between the raw poison of poverty
& the refined poison of wealth
our life together—
a small neutral country of happiness
Switzerland of the heart—
your secret-weapon smile
defending our borders from the darkness

3

in the non-Euclidean universe
of our love
all lines, straight or curved,
parallel or intersecting
lead from you to me,
me to you & back—
all points are mapped
equally onto both our lives—
all theorems about
true love are true—
& you & I
are the only axioms.

DAILY MIRACLES

Your breathing beside me in the night
The sequined velvet drum of stars
The slow-motion migration of stars
            heading west, never stopping
Moments of color: briefly pink clouds
in a stormy sky, a never-the-same sky
The daily drama of clouds sun wind
Range after range of peaks
A lake filling the horizon, west to east
            and beyond, our lake
The turquoise backdrop of so much love
The fortress of our love in a troubled world
The safe harbor of our house, our bed
            anchored to solid marble bedrock
A *laura* tree that never cracks in the wind
The second sunrise of your smile

*27 January 2010*

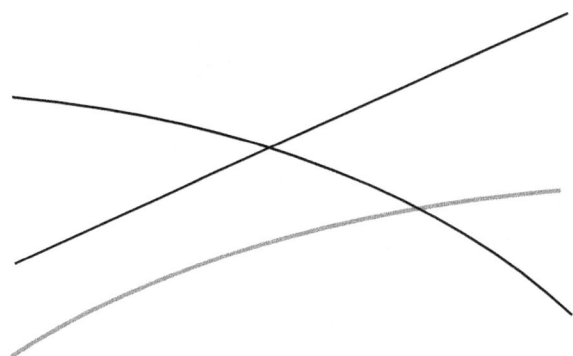

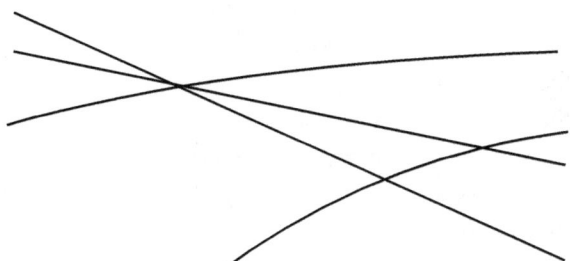

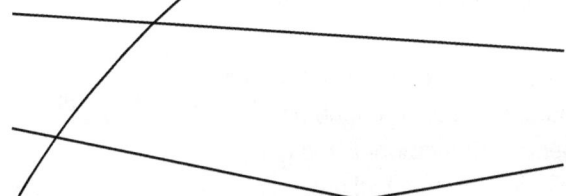

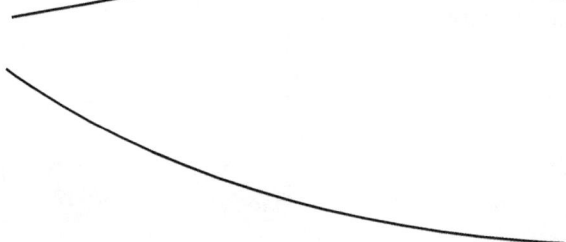

# STILL CRAZY IN LOVE

No longer raining, no longer even night,
But not yet day, dawn light spreading
Across the sky, trying for a rosy pink.
Way off west, at cloud cluttered horizon,
The full moon falls off the edge of the sky
Slipping down behind shadow peaks
The moon path rolled up and put away
Our lake now waiting for its share of color
Our lake? Why not? Our sky. Our moon.
Our memories of other moons, memories
Of other memories falling off the edges
Of other skies, other years, other lovers
Also called Lito and Linde, with their own
Memories of other Litos and Lindes,
Memories tumbled into the dusty closet
Beneath the edge of the sky. How many?
How many years ago did we meet?
How many wake-up kisses, cups of coffee?
Questions without answers, too many
To count, no need to count, no time
To spend with memories, today is waiting
And we're still here, still together,
Still waking up in time to applaud the dawn,
Still crazy in love.


*26 March 2011*
*Casa Mármol, Lago Carrera, Chile*

ENVOI

One more book
in a world
crowded with books

One more day
in a life
overflowing with days

One more chance
to say
how much I love you

*Liv.*

www.ingramcontent.com/pod-product-compliance
Lightning Source LLC
Chambersburg PA
CBHW071015040426

42443CB00007B/780